REVELATION
AND
VIOLENCE:

A Study in Contextualization

The 1986 Père Marquette
Theology Lecture

REVELATION
AND
VIOLENCE:

A Study in Contextualization

by

DR. WALTER BRUEGGEMANN

Professor of Old Testament
Eden Theological Seminary
St. Louis, Missouri

MARQUETTE UNIVERSITY PRESS
MILWAUKEE, WISCONSIN 53233

Library of Congress Catalogue Card Number: 86-060473

© Copyright 1986
Marquette University Press

ISBN 0-87462-541-6

Preface

The 1986 Père Marquette Lecture is the seventeenth in a series inaugurated to celebrate the Tercentenary of the missions and explorations of Père Marquette, S.J. (1637-1675). The Marquette University Theology Department, founded in 1952, launched these annual lectures by distinguished theologians under the title of the Père Marquette Lectures in 1969. The 1986 Lecture has the distinction of being the first event in the year long celebration of Marquette's twenty-five years of experience in graduate theology, the doctoral and master's degree programs, which were the outgrowth of a solidly academic undergraduate structure.

The 1986 lecture was delivered at Marquette University, April 20, 1986, by Dr. Walter Brueggemann, Professor of Old Testament, Eden Theological Seminary, St. Louis, Missouri.

Dr. Brueggemann holds a Th.D. (Old Testament) from Union Theological Seminary and a Ph.D. (Education) from St. Louis University. His sabbatical studies have taken him to the Universities of Heidelberg and Cambridge.

The American theological community is familiar with Dr. Brueggemann's service as a member of the Editorial Council of the *Journal of Biblical Literature,* Advisory Council of *Interpretation,* and the Executive Committee of the Association of Theological Schools. He is the founding editor of the series "Overtures to Biblical Theology" from Fortress Press.

Dr. Brueggemann's books include *The Bible Makes Sense* (1977), *The Land* (1977), *The Prophetic Imagination* (1978), *Genesis* (1982), *Praying the Psalms* (1982), *The Creative Word* (1982), *I Kings* and *II Kings* (1983), and *David's Truth in Israel's Imagination & Memory* (1985). He has published numerous articles in national and international scholarly journals.

The works of Dr. Brueggemann generally are representative of current trends in Old Testament scholarship and form part of the cutting edge of contemporary research. His knowledge of new directions and findings make his work treasure-troves of information and insight. This lecture makes use of two recently honed methods of biblical scholarship – sociological reading and literary analysis – and applies them to Joshua 11, a passage that has been a problem for many who look to the Bible to give life.

REVELATION AND VIOLENCE:
A Study in Contextualization

The conviction that scripture is revelatory literature is a constant, abiding conviction among the communities of Jews and Christians which gather around the book.[1] But that conviction, constant and abiding as it is, is problematic and open to a variety of alternative and often contradictory or ambiguous meanings.[2] Clearly that conviction is appropriated differently in various contexts and various cultural settings.[3] Current attention to hermeneutics convinces many of us that there is no single, sure meaning for any text. The revelatory power of the text is discerned and given precisely through the action of interpretation which is always concrete, never universal, always contextualized, never "above the fray," always filtered through vested interest, never in disinterested purity.[4]

If that is true for the interpretive end of the process which *receives the text,* we may entertain the notion that it is also true for the interpretive end of the process which *forms,* shapes and offers the text. That is, not only in its hearing, but also in its speaking, the text makes its disclosure in ways that are concrete, contextualized, and filtered through vested interest. While this leaves open the charge of relativism, it is in fact only a candid acknowledgement of the central conviction around which historical-critical studies have revolved for 200 years. Historical-critical studies have insisted that a text can only be understood in context. Historical-critical study believes historical context is necessary to hearing the text. But our objectivist ideology has uncritically insisted that knowledge of historical context of a text would let us be objective interpreters without recognizing that from its very inception, the textual process is not and cannot be objective.[5]

Historical-critical study thus gives us access to a certain interpretive act which generates the text, but that original interpretive act is not objective. This acknowledgement of the formation of the text as a constructive event is a recognition of what we know about ourselves, that we are not only meaning receivers, but we are also meaning makers. We not only accept meanings offered, but we construct meanings which we advocate.[6] The receiving, constructing act of interpretation changes both us and the text. This suggests that scripture as revelation is never simply a final disclosure, but is an ongoing act of disclosing which will never let the disclosure be closed. The disclosing process is an open interaction with choices exercised in every step of interpretation from formation to reception.

I

The emergence of two more or less new methods of scripture interpretation is important for the relation between revelation and interpretation. In this lecture I want to consider both of these methods in relation to the revelatory character of the text.

The first of these methods is sociological.[7] It has become apparent that much historical-critical study has focused on the question of facticity to so large an extent that it has bracketed out questions of social process, social interest, and social possibility. A

number of recent studies have made use of
tools of social analysis to ask about the social
intention and social function of a text in relation to the community and the situation upon
which the text impinges. [8] Among the more
important of these studies are Gottwald on
the early period, [9] Wilson on the prophets, [10]
and Hanson on the later period. [11] A program-
matic formula for such an enterprise is that
it is a "materialist" reading, [12] a phrase Gottwald would accept for his work, but perhaps
Wilson and Hanson would not. A "materialist
reading" suggests that the text cannot be
separated from the social processes out of
which it emerged. The text also is a product
of the community. The community which
generates the text is engaged in production
of the text and the community which reads
it is engaged in consumption of the text, so
that the text needs to be discussed according
to processes of production and consumption. [13]
In what follows, I will want to consider a
materialist reading of a text, as an attempt
to appropriate its revelatory claim. The text
as product for consumption suggests the
operation of intentionality and interest in the
shaping of the text.

The second emerging method which will be useful for us is literary analysis. Literary analysis seeks to take the text on its own terms as an offer of meaning, as an exercise in creative imagination to construct a world that does not exist apart from the literary act of the text.[14] The nuances of the text are not simply imaginative literary moves, but are acts of world-making which create and evoke an alternative world available only through this text. The authoritative voices in such a method are Paul Ricoeur[15] and Amos Wilder.[16] In Old Testament studies, among the more effective efforts at analyses of literature as "making worlds" are those of David Gunn,[17] and David Clines[18] and Phyllis Trible.[19]

This literary approach seeks to receive the world offered in the text, even if that world is distant from and incongruent with our own. Thus the text is not a report on a world "out there," but is an offer of another world that is evoked in and precisely by the text. The text "reveals" a world that would not be disclosed apart from this text. This view suggests that the alternative to the world of this text is not an objective world out there, but it is another "evoked world"[20] from another text, albeit a text which may be invisible and unrecognized by us. We are always choosing between texts, and the interpretive act is to see the ways in which the world disclosed in this text is a compelling "sense-making" world.[21] Literary analysis assumes that the text is not a one-dimensional statement, but is an offer of a world that has an interiority, in which the text is not a monolithic voice, but is a conversation out of which comes a new world.

When one puts the sociological and literary methods together in a common interpretive act,[22] it is clear that the voices in the text may speak and be heard and interpreted in various ways. Some voices may be shrill and domineering, some may be willingly quiet, some may be silenced and defeated. It is, nonetheless, the entire conversation in the text that discloses an alternative world for us. Thus scripture as revelation is not a flat, obvious offer of a conclusion, but it is an ongoing conversation which evokes, invites and offers. It is the process of the text itself, in which each interpretive generation participates, that is the truth of revelation. Such an interaction is not a contextless activity but the context is kept open and freshly available, depending on the social commitments of the interpreter and the sense-making conversations heard in the act of interpretation. In this strange interpretive process, we dare to claim and confess that God's fresh word and new truth are mediated and made available to us.

II

To pursue this matter of "revelation in context," I will address an exceedingly hard text in the Old Testament, Joshua 11. The reason for taking up this text is to deal with the often asked and troublesome question, what shall we do with all the violence and bloody war that is done in the Old Testament in the name of Yahweh?[23] The question reflects a sense that these texts of violence are at least an embarrassment, are morally repulsive, and are theologically problematic in the Bible, not because they are violent, but because this is violence either in the name of or at the hand of Yahweh.

The question we shall consider is: How are these texts of violence to be understood as

revelation? What is it that is disclosed and
how shall this disclosure be received as serious, authoritative, and binding as the only
rule for life and faith? We shall consider the
revelatory question in two dimensions. The
first is revelation *within* the text. What has
drawn me to Joshua 11 is the awareness that
within the text as such very little, surprisingly
little, is directly assigned to Yahweh as revelation. So we ask how the characters in this
text discerned God's revelation. Second, we
shall go on to ask about how *the whole of the
text* is taken as revelation, once the text is
stabilized for us. It may well be that this distinction will be useful in understanding how
this text should be handled in faith communities which celebrate revelation, but flinch
from violence linked to God. The warrant for
violence within the text may yield a very
different disclosure when the text is taken by
us as a stable revelatory unit. In our text what
Joshua and ancient Israel took as revelation
may provide a clue for our hearing the text
as revelatory. But the two may not be identified or equated.

III

We may begin with a summary of some standard critical observations.[24] The first half of the book of Joshua, chapters 1-12, concerns the conquest of the land which is done by God, whereas 13-22 concerns the division of the land, done by Joshua. The book of Joshua is a theological account in which God acts directly as an agent in the narrative. Within chapters 1-12, the specific narrative accounts concern,

Joshua 2 and 6: the conquest of Jericho,
   3 and 4: the crossing at Gilgal,
   5: the institution of circumcision,
   7 and 8:1-29: the crisis of Achan and Ai,
   8:30-35: the altar at Schechem,
   9: the subservience of the Gibeonites,
   10: the taking of the south.

Alt has suggested that these narratives conclude with aitiological formulae which evidence that they were originally teaching tales to justify present phenomena. He has observed that these aitiological narratives tend to be located in a narrow geographical range with particular reference to the tribal area of Benjamin.[25]

Chapters 1, 11:16-23, and 12 are more general statements which make more sweeping claims. It seems apparent that chapters 1 and 12 are placed as a theological envelope for the more specific accounts. Chapter 11 tends to move toward a comprehensive summary (vv. 16-23), but focuses on the specific matter of Hazor, the great city of the north (vv. 1-15). [26] Thus it has affinities with the generalizations of 12, but also balances the southern account of 10 with this northern report on Hazor. [27] To the extent that this chapter generalizes, it may also reflect Deuteronomic stylization.

Within Chapter 11 we may present an overview of the following elements:

1. In vv. 1-5 the king of Hazor takes the initiative in mobilizing many other kings to resist Israel. It is important that in this case it is not Israel who is the aggressor. [28] The inventory of mobilized kings must be a generalized and stylized list. It includes kings of the north, kings of the south, and nations that characteristically occur in the sterotypical Deuteronomic list of seven nations (Deut. 7:1; 20:17). Thus the list is not to be taken as historically literal. What interests us about the list is that it reflects the power of city states, armed with "many horses and chariots." Following the general analysis of Gottwald, [29]

the city states are to be understood as monopolies of socio-economic, political power which are managed in hierarchal and oppressive ways. "Horses and chariots" reflect the strength and monopoly of arms that are necessary and available for the maintenance of the economic and political monopoly.[30]

2. Vv. 16-20[31] is a summary that roughly corresponds to the summary of vv. 1-5. There (vv. 1-5) we have the list of enemies of Israel. Here (vv. 16-20) we are told that Joshua defeated all of them.

3. Vv. 21-23 is concerned with a special observation about the Anakim who were defeated, except in cities assigned to Philistia. This section, according to Noth, is Dtr. It makes a transition to the distribution of land in what follows, and it ends with the standard formula about rest in the land. Thus in vv. 1-5, 16-23 we have sweeping generalizations that frame the chapter which is built around an older story. There has been a great effort against Israel who, with the intervention of Yahweh, has won, even against enormous odds.

4. In vv. 6-9 we have the central narrative element of the text, the command of Yahweh (v. 6), the responsive action of Joshua (vv. 7-8),

and the concluding formula that Joshua obeyed the command of Yahweh (v. 9). This unit is of particular interest because v. 6 is the only speech of Yahweh in the entire chapter and indeed the only speech from anyone. All the rest is narrative. For our interest in revelation, we may expect that this speech element will be of particular importance.

5. In vv. 10-15 we have a battle report concerning the actual conquest of Hazor, whose king made the initial move toward war in v. 1. These verses are of special interest, as Polzin has seen, because of the settlement made on the traditional command of *ḥerem*. [32]

Thus chap. 11 is framed by a general summary (vv. 1-5, 16-23). The latter part of the envelope may not all be of a piece, but it is all summary. Inside the framework are two much more specific statements which concern us, vv. 6-9 on command and obedience, and vv. 10-15 on the destruction of Hazor and the problem of *ḥerem*. Even though the chapter tends to be handled as a generalizing conclusion, there is little here that is specifically Deuteronomistic. The parts that concern us stand largely free of that influence, except perhaps the formula of obedience in v. 10.

IV

In the invitation for this lecture, both professors who wrote me suggested that I deal with the sociology of the monarchal period. I hope it will be clear to you that I have taken that suggestion seriously, even if not directly. I understand monarchy in Israel, or among its neighbors, to be a political concentration of power and an economic monopoly of wealth. When monarchy appears in Israel, it comes along with such concentration and monopoly, though of course there are important models available for royal Israel prior to David and Solomon. Such concentrations and monopolies have to be maintained and therefore defended, because such monopoly is not welcomed by everyone, especially those who are disadvantaged by it and exploited for it. Interestingly, Gottwald[33] has suggested that the formation of the monarchy (so disputed in I Sam. 7-15) is not simply defense against the Philistines, as is a conventional view among us, but is the necessary and predictable political counterpart of a growing economic surplus and monopoly. That is, the state did not gather the surplus, but the accu-

mulated, disproportionate surplus necessi-
tated the state in order to legitimate, maintain and protect a surplus which was already
partly in hand.

In Joshua 11, of course, we have no Israelite monarchy. But we do have monarchies
which in this narrative are antagonistic to
Israel. Following the model of Gottwald, I
regard "Israel" as an egalitarian, peasant
movement hostile to every concentration,
surplus, and monopoly. Conversely it follows
then that every such city-state as those listed
in vv. 1-5 would regard Israel as a threat, for
Israel practiced a social alternative which
must be destroyed. Thus we can read the
mobilization of the Hazor king with sociological realism as a conflict between competing
social systems.[34] The initative of the king of
Hazor is preemptive, perhaps not unlike the
U.S. initiative against the alleged growing
threat of the Sandinistas in Nicaragua.

We may begin our textual analysis by not-
ing the three-fold reference to "horses and
chariots" in this narrative. First, in v. 4, the
military mobilization of city-states is routinely
described as "horses and chariots." Israel has
none, for horses and chariots are tools of

states and empires, necessary and paid for in order to guard the monopoly. That is a given in this ancient society.

In v. 6, "horses and chariots" are mentioned a second time, this time in a statement by Yahweh:

> Do not be afraid of them, for tomorrow at this time I will give over all of them slain to Israel. You shall hamstring the horses and burn the chariots with fire.

This is a remarkably interesting speech.[35] First it is an assurance, "do not fear." It is as though Yahweh recognizes how dangerous the situation is for Israel, because the military contest is a hopeless mismatch. It is an uneven match because the city-states have advanced military technology and Israel has no access to such technology. The only counter to military technology, according to the narrative, is the powerful liberating voice of Yahweh. Second, as often following "do not fear," there is a promise of a quite specific kind, introduced by *kî* "tomorrow I am giving them over to you slain."[36] Third, after the promise and the assurance is the command, with the word order inverted, forming a chiasmus with the promise for accent:

> Their horses you will hamstring,
>   their chariots you will burn in fire.

This speech (v. 6) is at the center of our
interest in revelation, for it is God's only
speech in this chapter. This speech, including
assurance, promise and command, is address-
ed only to Joshua the leader, not the troops
as in Deut. 20:2-4. All of the real action in this
unit is to be done by Israelites, who are to
sabotage and immobilize the imperial weapons of war. Yahweh undertakes no direct
action. We should note that in this direct command, the only object of violence is horses and
chariots, i.e., weapons. There is nothing here
about burning cities, killing kings or people,
nor seizing war booty. Yahweh's is a very lean
mandate which addresses the simple, most
important issue, the military threat of monarchal power against this alternative community lacking in military technology.

What we may most wonder about is what
it is exactly that Yahweh promises to do.
After the assurance and the rather nonspe-
cific participle ("I am giving"), Yahweh does
nothing, but mandates Israel to do the action.
I submit that a close reading shows Yahweh
really does nothing in this verse and indeed
does not promise to do anything beyond a
general commitment of solidarity and legiti-

mation. The action is left to Joshua and to Israel.

The third reference to "horses and chariots" (v. 9) reports that Joshua did as commanded and destroyed the military weapons of the military city-states. Thus there are three references to horses and chariots:

The city kings had them (v. 4),
Yahweh mandates their destruction (v. 6),
Joshua destroys them as commanded (v. 9).

The first and third references are factual and descriptive, before and after the war. The second, in the mouth of Yahweh, is wondrously unlike the other two mentions. It is the speech of Yahweh. Here the text is not historically descriptive but theologically evocative. The disclosure is that Yahweh gave permission for Joshua and Israel to act for their justice and liberation against an oppressive adversary. This revelatory word of Yahweh, given directly without conduit or process, is only authorization for a liberating movement which is sure to be violent, but only violent against weapons. We do not know by what means this word has been given and received and the narrative has no interest in that.

The best guess is that it was an oracle to an officer, but that is to speculate outside the narrative presentation. But we do know that the disclosure of permit was taken seriously, not doubted, regarded as valid and acted upon. What is revealed is that Yahweh is allied with the marginalized, oppressed peasants against the monopoly of the city-state. It is not a summons to violence (though its practice might be construed so) but only a permit[37] that Joshua's community is entitled to dream, hope and imagine freedom and is entitled to act upon that dream, hope and imagination.

Now our focal question is to ask, would the God of the Bible make such a disclosure as a permit for liberation which entailed violence against oppressive weapons and, by inference, against the systems which sanction such weapons?

1. We are bound to say that such a revelatory word is congruent with the fabric of Exodus faith, for Yahweh is there presented as a force for justice and liberation against concentrations of oppressive power. Yahweh's commitment is summarized in the slogan, "Let my people go" (Ex. 5:1, 7:16, 8:1, 20, 9:1, 13, 10:3).

2. The disclosure of Yahweh is not intervention, but authorization. The claim of the narrative here is exceedingly modest. How indeed is liberation to happen in such a context? Israel, according to this narrative, is not recipient of a supernatural intervention. If justice and freedom are to come, Yahweh's way is through actual historical agents who act on their own behalf. That is what the text narrates. This rather obvious fact is of exceeding importance for the general interpretive posture taken here.

3. The authorization is the authorization of Joshua, his leadership, and his strategy. No one else has access to the disclosure. No one else heard the disclosure. No one else knows what was said. Revelation is linked to authorized communal authority, or in other categories, the revelation is the property of the agents that hold a monopoly of interpretation. [38]

4. The disclosure from God that authorizes coheres with the dreams and yearning of this oppressed community, has credibility only in that community, and cannot be removed from that community for a more general statement. It was Israel's longstanding and courageous dream of an alternative

social organization rooted in the memory of Moses that is the material and mode out of which revelation is articulated. Once this community has glimpsed the imaginative possibility of justice which it had glimpsed in the Exodus, it could not understand itself unauthorized by God's disclosure. The disclosure that authorizes lives very close to the actual experience of the community. That is, revelation is not an act extrinsic to the social process but it is an act precisely embedded in the social community.[39]

Instead of suggesting that revelation comes down to intrude in the community, I submit that this revelation arises up out of the hurt and the hope of this community, so that the dream is understood as certified from heaven, and as that dream is certified from heaven, it has enormous credibility in the life of the community on earth. The dream of liberation and justice has credibility theologically because to deny it is to deny everything Israel knows about Yahweh, the Lord of the Exodus. The revelatory word has credibility sociologically because the certitude of disclosure is not simply religious certitude, but a much more embedded, visceral, existential certitude that would not be denied. Israel knows deep in its own hurt and hope that this permit is God's truth and God's will.

Revelation for this community in the text is the convergence of the *old memory of liberation* from the Exodus,[40] *the peasant yearning* for liberation and justice,[41] and the *formal speech reported by established leadership.* All three elements are indispensable. The disclosure cannot be denied because passion for liberating justice cannot be denied Yahweh who is known in the Exodus tradition. The disclosure cannot be denied because the future social possibility is now unleashed in peasant imagination and will not be nullified. The disclosure cannot be denied because the authorization is reported on the lips of the authorized leader, Joshua, who is understood as fulfilling the function of Moses. The outcome is that no monarchal "horses and chariots" are permitted to stand in the way of such a promise from heaven or such a possibility on earth. All three elements, memory, yearning and leadership converge in this permit of Yahweh.

The revelatory speech of Yahweh ends this way: "Hamstring the horses, burn the chariots

with fire." When God speaks, we may expect
something more respectable, something about
"This is my beloved son," or "Three persons
and one substance," or "Grace alone, scripture
alone, Christ alone." But here it is "hamstring
the horses."

In a classic essay, H.R. Niebuhr has seen
that revelation is embedded in community. [42]
John McKenzie has argued more specifically
the same way. [43] Both Niebuhr and McKenzie
have seen that revelation and inspiration arise
as a certitude given and received in a community. But it is characteristic of that generation of scholarship represented by Niebuhr
and McKenzie that the notion of communities
of revelation is understood without adequate
reference to specific sociological circum-
stance. [44] That is, if communities mediate
revelation from God, surely different communities in different circumstances will
mediate different disclosures. The community
of the king of Hazor must have mediated
God's intent for greater armed security. But
to the community of Israel (understood as a
community of marginality) which has given
us this text we claim as revelatory, what
God discloses is a permit or authorization to

demobilize such royal arms which are threats to human welfare and specifically to the welfare of this community of marginality. If revelation is mediated through community, revelation will reflect the truth available to that community in its life, memory and experience, and will tend therefore to be partisan disclosure. I submit that this community of oppressed peasants through which the winds of liberation blow could not mediate any other revelation from God and could not doubt this disclosure. The high God of eternity dwells with the lowly (Is. 57:15-16). For that reason, the God of these tribes decrees hamstringing horses as one concrete practice of truth. The truth of the disclosure is that it makes life possible for the community.

Except for Yahweh's permit and mandate in v. 6, all action in the narrative is left to Joshua and Israel. In their obedience to and trust in Yahweh's permit, Joshua and Israel do everything that is needful, while Yahweh does nothing. It is clear that Yahweh in fact does not "act" in this narrative, except in the important sense that the entire event occurs as Yahweh's act. [45] Yahweh made a promise in v.6: "I will give over." In v. 8 that promise is kept: "And Yahweh gave them into the hand of Israel." We are not told what Yahweh did nor how it was done. Evidently Yahweh has authorized and legitimated, and that was enough. Even in v. 20 where the rhetoric is escalated, Yahweh does not act in a concrete way. Thus I suggest that revelation in this narrative is not self-disclosure of God, for nothing new is shown of God, but revelation is the gift of authorization by which Joshua and Israel are legitimated for their own acts of liberation, which from the side of the king of Hazor are perceived as acts of violence. What is "dis-closed" is that the world of the city-kings is not closed. It is the purpose of "horses and chariots" to close that world and so to render the peasants hopeless and helpless.[46] But the world ostensibly controlled by oppressive city-kings is now dis-closed, shown to be false and broken open to the joy of Israel. The revelatory decree of Yahweh breaks the fixed world of city-kings. What we label as violence on Yahweh's part is a theological permit which sanctions a new social possibility.

That single, simple act of authorization is, religiously speaking, everything. It permits

Israel to act. The main verbs of this chapter, therefore, have Israel, not Yahweh, as subject:

> They fell upon them (v. 7).
> They smote (vv. 8, 10, 14, 17).
> They utterly destroyed (vv. 11, 12, 20, 21).

The word of Yahweh, given only to Joshua, created new historical, social possibilities for Israel, out of which Israel was able to act. The result is the complete transformation of the power situation of the world of Israel, a transformation wrought by the direct active intervention of Israel, not of Yahweh.

This is not to make a liberal claim that "God has no hands but ours." Yahweh does the one thing needful. Yahweh legitimates self-assertion on the part of the powerless. The juxtaposition of God's power and human power needs to be nuanced very differently among those with horses and chariots. But this is not their text.

V

The simple sequence of statements on horses and chariots (vv. 4, 6, 9) is unambiguous. Horses and chariots are a threat to the social experiment which is Israel. Horses and

chariots are unqualifiedly bad and unalterably
condemned. They symbolize and embody oppression. They function only to impose harsh
control on some by others. They must be
destroyed. Yahweh authorizes their destruction. Joshua and Israel act in obedience to
Yahweh's sovereign command and destroy
them. Horses and chariots, according to this
narrative, have no positive, useful purpose in
the world of ancient Israel, for they serve only
to maintain the status quo in which some
dominate others. Israel as a liberated community of the Exodus has no need for such
a mode of social power. [47] Moreover Yahweh
is the sworn enemy of such modes of power.

Israel's sense of cattle, in this narrative
and generally, is very different. Cattle are
never instruments of war or oppression. They
may be a measure of affluence (Gen. 32:15,
Jonah 4:11), but they only serve as meat and
milk, for domestic and communal well-being.
Because they are not symbols of domination
and oppression as are horses and chariots, a
simple social analysis of cattle is not adequate.
In his close reading of Joshua 11, Polzin has
discerned a certain playful ambiguity in the
narrative concerning cattle and their disposi-

tion, an ambiguity that Israel does not have about horses and chariots.[48] Because cattle are not sociologically unambiguous for Israel as are horses and chariots, Israel's sense of Yahweh's will concerning cattle also is not unambiguous. Horses are clearly for domination. But cattle may either be seductive or sustaining, and so Yahweh's will for their treatment requires more careful nuanced attention.

We have seen that v. 6 gives an unambiguous command on horses and chariots. They are to be destroyed. Concerning cattle and other spoil, however, the narrative departs from the command of v. 6 in two contrasting directions.

1. A total and massive destruction is commanded, a *more harsh* destruction than that authorized in v. 6:

   a) *Ḥerem* is practiced, "as Moses the servant of the Lord had commanded" (v. 12).

   b) Cattle are taken as spoil, but every man is smote, "as the Lord had commanded Moses his servant, so Moses commanded Joshua, so Joshua did;

he left nothing undone of all that the Lord had commanded Moses" (v. 15).

c) *Ḥerem* is practiced again. "It was the Lord's doing to harden their hearts that they should come against Israel in battle in order that they should be utterly destroyed and should receive no mercy, but be exterminated, as the Lord commanded Moses" (v. 20).

d) The whole land is seized, "So Joshua took the whole land, according to all that the Lord had spoken to Moses . . . and the land had rest" (v. 23).

Two things are striking about these statements. First, they are not the direct speech of Yahweh, in contrast to v. 6, but are attributed to Moses in a former generation. Yahweh speaks directly about horses and chariots, but only indirectly through Moses about cattle and spoil. The command (and therefore the revelation) is remembered revelation:

As Moses had commanded (v. 12),
So Moses commanded Joshua (v. 15),
Yahweh commanded Moses (v. 20),
The Lord had spoken to Moses (v. 23).

Because the revelation is an unspecified reference to older torah, the community of necessity must interpret. Which older torah teaching is invoked is not self-evident, nor exactly how it applies to this situation. This means that with regard to cattle and spoil, there is room for speculation, maneuverability and alternative decisions.

Second, these mandates which are attributed to Yahweh through the memory of Moses are exceedingly harsh, not as disciplined, specific, and restrained as the command of v. 6:

> to utterly destroy (v. 12),
> not to leave any that breathed (v. 14),
> utterly destroyed, no mercy, exterminated (v. 20),
> take the whole land (v. 23).

In each case an old textual warrant (presumably Deut. 20:15-18) is claimed as authorization for the present destruction. That old textual warrant is remembered and presented as uncompromisingly harsh.

2. But in Joshua 11, as Polzin has observed, the command regarding other spoil is also *more lenient* than the mandate regarding horses and chariots. The command of v. 6 is a harsh command. But as the narrative

develops and horses and chariots are to be
destroyed, cattle may be taken and saved as
booty (Josh. 11:14). It is curious that in the
very text which urges that "nothing be left
breathing," cattle are exempted. The enact-
ment of God's mandate is contextualized by
Israel.

The harsh remembered demand of Moses
and the permit of Moses to take spoil (cf.
Deut. 20:14) both depart from v. 6, the former
in a more demanding direction, the latter in
a more lenient direction.

Both the harshness and the leniency are
based on the old torah memory of Deuteronomy, in 20:10-14 and 20:15-18 respectively.
Based on the old torah memory, in the name
of Moses our narrative practices both extermination and spoil, both radical rejection of
booty and economic prudence, both obedient
destruction and self-serving confiscation.
Both are warranted by the torah teaching of
Deut. 20, a polarity Polzin has not allowed.

I take v. 6, Yahweh's only direct speech
in Josh. 11, as the normative revelation within
the text. It mandates destruction of a quite
specific kind in order to give liberated Israel
room to exist. It sanctions neither more nor

less than this. In two ways the narrative around v. 6 departs from this normative mandate. On the one hand, in vv. 7-8 Israel did *much more* than is authorized: "Israel fell . . . smote . . . pursued . . . smote . . . until they left none remaining." They killed people and destroyed cities, surely not decreed by Yahweh in v. 6. On the other hand, one may say they did *less,* for they took cattle as booty, also not authorized by v. 6. One might construe v. 6 as a directive to immobilize anything held by the hostile city-states, but that is not subsequently understood to include cattle.

The narrative of Josh. 11 thus may be sorted out at three levels:

1. Theologically, there is a distinction between what is to be exterminated and what is to be kept as spoil, even though the decree of v. 6 authorizes neither spoil nor extermination. Both extermination and spoil are warranted in the torah tradition of Deut. 20, spoil in vv. 10-14 and extermination in vv. 15-17. [49]

2. Sociologically there is a distinction between horses (and chariots) and cattle (and other spoil). Horses and cattle symbolize very different things and perform very different

social functions. Horses function to dominate because they are a means of military power. Cattle function to sustain by providing meat and milk. Horses can never provide sustenance. Cattle can never aid in oppression.

3. Methodologically there is a distinction between sociological and literary analysis. Thus I have used only sociological methods to ask what horse and chariot symbolize and what social functions they perform and why Yahweh wills their immobilization. To ask a question of the social symbolization and function of horse and chariot leads to something like a "class reading" of the matter, for clearly horse and chariot are tools of domination.

On the other hand, (following Polzin) reference to cattle and spoil has evoked subtle literary questions because we are able to see how the tradition struggles with the tension of spoil and extermination, how cattle require a more subtle sorting out than does the socially unambiguous reality of horses. We are able to see that the revelatory operation within the narrative is indeed subtle and requires careful differentiations. Thus horses as tool and symbol of domination permit a clear, unambiguous announcement of God's will.

Cattle which may be a means of seduction (Deut. 20:15-18) or a means of sustenance (Deut. 20:14-15) require a more delicate articulation of God's will. It will not do simply to ask about "all that violence," because the situation of the text is much more complicated than that. The warrant for violence is grounded in v. 6. One may imagine that Israel took that limited, disciplined warrant of Yahweh and went well beyond its intent or substance in its action, out of rage and oppression. [50] The action against the horses is based on a revelatory permit for liberation. The sanction for keeping cattle looks to the future just community which will replace the oppressive city-states.

What we have, then, is revelation in context. The popular way of putting the question is, Would the God of the Bible mandate such violence? But the question must be posed in context. Of the remembered revelation rooted in the memory of Moses, the answer is "yes," in the interest of Israel's survival as a holy people (Deut. 7:6). Of the immediate revelation, the answer is "yes," as a means of eliminating implements of domination. But I do not want to evade our governing question.

Does God mandate violence? Properly contextualized, this narrative answers "yes," but of a specific kind, tightly circumscribed, in the interest of a serious social experiment, in the interest of ending domination. The revelation is not really act, but warrant or permit. The narrative requires us to conclude that this community was utterly persuaded that the God of the tradition is passionately against domination and is passionately for an egalitarian community.

It is futile to try to talk such a community of the oppressed out of such a theological conviction. Its certitude does not arise out of religious rumination, but out of the visceral sense of pain and oppression which is the stuff of history. This community of Israel, however we articulate its sociology of marginality, knows deep in its bones that God did not intend long-term subservience. Perhaps that conviction came by the bearers of the news of the Exodus, [51] but I suggest it came in their particular context of oppression. The conviction of God's disclosure is linked to that context. Its actual implementation of extermination, hamstringing and taking spoil is also given in the matrix of social practice, not

apart from it. Questions about violence authorized by God must be kept very close to the
visceral hurt and hope of such communities
of marginality. It is remarkable that the judgment and certitude of such a community has
been received by us as canonical, but it has
indeed been so received.

The matter of revelation inside the narrative finally requires comment on v. 20:

> It was the Lord's doing to harden their hearts that
> they should come against Israel in battle, in order
> that they should be utterly destroyed and should
> receive no mercy, but be exterminated, as the Lord
> commanded Moses.

The second half of the verse is controlled
by two uses of *lema'an:*

> In order that they should come against Israel...
> in order that they should be destroyed.

But the intriguing statement is, "It was
the Lord's doing to harden their hearts."[52]
What I find interesting about this statement
is the question of knowledge: How did Israel
know this? How did Israel decide Yahweh did
it? The statement does not claim Yahweh was
in the battle, but only that Yahweh worked
to convene the battle so that there would be

a victory. This is a marvelously elusive theological formula to juxtapose to the concreteness of v. 6. God is not immediately involved in any direct way, but Israel knows that governance is finally in Yahweh's hands as was the case in the remembered Exodus (Ex. 4:21, 7:3, 9:12, 10:1). The conclusion drawn in v. 20 asserts the majestic, irresistible sovereignty of Yahweh. But that grand claim of sovereignty finally rests on the concreteness of v. 6. Without the concreteness of v. 6, the claim of v. 20 is without substance.

VI

Now we may turn to the second question of revelation, the disclosure given by the narrative as narrative, not to its own participants, but to us who now stand outside the narrative, take it as canonical, and heed it as revelatory. A good test is to ask, what would we know of the ways and character of God if we had only this particular rendering, or what would be lost if we did not have this text?

I have proposed that Yahweh's command in v. 6 is theologically normative. It is not as harsh as general extermination. It is not as lenient as taking spoil. This theologically normative disclosure concerns Yahweh's hostility to horses and chariots which are monarchal instruments of domination.[53] These instruments of domination a) require advanced technology, b) require surplus wealth to finance and maintain, and c) serve a political, economic monopoly dependent on oppression and subservience. We have ample evidence to suggest the social function of horses and chariots for kings. In the inventory of Solomon's affluence and security, he is said to have 40,000 stalls of horses for his chariots and 12,000 horsemen (I Kings 4:26). In 10:26, it is reported "Solomon gathered together chariots and horsemen; he had fourteen hundred chariots and twelve thousand horsemen," partly for trade, but mostly for defense and intimidation.[54] The Bible characteristically associates horses and chariots with royal power which is regularly seen to be oppressive (cf. Ex. 14:9, 23, Deut. 20:1, II Sam. 15:1, I Kings 18:5, 22:4, II Kings 3:7, 18:23, 23:11).

Yahweh's hostility to horses and chariots bespeaks Yahweh's hostility to the social system which requires, legitimates, and depends upon them. Israel, in its early period of tribal-peasant life, did not have horses and chariots and greatly feared them. The struggle reflected in Joshua 11 is how this community, so vulnerable and helpless, can exist and function against the kings and their powerful tools of domination.

In light of the inventory of the royal use of horses and chariots, we now consider an alternative set of texts expressed in a very different mode which present a critical view of horses and chariots. These narrative accounts are in a sense expository comments on the sanction of Josh. 11:6.

The Bible is not content simply to describe the royal status quo which seems beyond challenge. The Bible also offers tales of liberation which show Israel challenging, countering and overcoming this formidable royal power. The narrative form lends itself to the articulation of another kind of power which the royal world neither knows nor credits.[55] The narrative mode challenges royal rationality even as the narrative substance challenges royal policy.

1. In I Kings 20, Israel is ranged against Syria in an uneven contest. The Syrians, a

prototype of military power, are sure of their strength:

> And the servants of the king of Syria said to him, "Their gods are gods of the hills, and so they were stronger than we; but let us fight against them in the plain, and surely we will be stronger than they... muster an army like the army that you have lost, horse for horse, and chariot for chariot; then we will fight against them in the plain, and surely we will be stronger than they" (20:23-25).

The Israelites, in their own narrative presentation, are helpless by contrast:

> And the people of Israel encamped before them like two little flocks of goats, but the Syrians filled the country (v. 27).

The narrative makes the disproportion of royal power clear. That in turn makes the victory of Yahweh all the more dramatic:

> Because the Syrians have said, "The Lord is a god of the hills but he is not a god of the valleys," therefore I will give all this great multitude into your hand, and you shall know that I am the Lord (v. 28).

The episode concludes with a great victory. Israel's God and Israel's narrators are undaunted by the odds of royal horses and chariots. They are undaunted because there is another power which overwhelms and over-

rides the royal establishment and gives victory to these seemingly helpless peasants.
Notice that at the crucial point of the narrative where we would want specificity we are
told nothing.[56] At the point where we would
like to know how Yahweh defeated the Syrian
horses and chariots, the narrative is opaque.
We are not told. It is enough to receive the
surprising news that is against the data. It
is enough to know that Yahweh triumphs over
the Syrian gods, and therefore Israel over
Syria, and therefore faith triumphs over
horses and chariots.

2. A second narrative which offers a cri-
tique of horses and chariots again concerns
Syria, Israel, and Elisha (II Kings 6:15-19).
Syria discerns that Elisha is the main threat
and sends "horses and chariots and a great
army" to seize him (II Kings 6:14). Israel's
prophet is in great danger and seemingly de-
fenseless. But the narrative focuses on the
faith of Elisha and the power of Yahweh.
First, Elisha issues a formal assurance: "Fear
not, for those who are with us are more than
those who are with them" (v. 16).[57] Second,
Elisha prays that frightened Israel, embodied
in his servant, may see (v. 17). And third, in

answer to the prayer, Yahweh causes the young man to see "And behold, the mountain was full of horses and chariots of fire round about Elisha" (v. 17). Again the narrative is elliptical just at the place where we would like to know more. It is enough for our purposes, however, to see that through the prophetic person, the power of prayer, and the courage of faith, Yahweh's powerful sovereignty is present in horses and chariots which effectively counter the Syrians (v. 17).

3. In a different episode of this same extended narrative, the motif of Yahweh's defeat of horses and chariots recurs (II Kings 7:3-8). Four lepers enter the camp of the Syrians, but the Syrians had all fled. Persons as socially irrelevant as lepers can safely enter the Syrian stronghold.

The narrative explanation for the flight of the Syrians is this:

> For the Lord had made the army of the Syrians hear the sound of chariots and horses, the sound of a great army, so that they said to one another, "Behold, the king of Israel has hired against us the kings of the Hittites and the kings of Egypt to come upon us." So they fled away in the twilight and forsook their tents, their horses and their asses, leaving the camp as it was, and fled for their lives (II Kings 7:6-7).

The narrative continues, saying that the
lepers seized spoil of silver, gold and clothing
(v. 8).[58] Again a victory is inscrutably won by
Yahweh against the great odds of the military
power of a foreign state. The mode of the victory is comic, whimsical or hidden. But it is
decisive. The Israelites had not hired allies as
Syria suspected (v. 6). Israel did not need
allies other than Yahweh. The narrator under-
stands this perfectly, but the marching Syrians have no access to the reality evoked by
this narrative. The narrative thus delegiti-
mates the rationality of Syrian royal power.

The outcome of all three narratives in I
Kings 20, II Kings 6 and 7 is that Yahweh is
shown to be stronger than the military state
and is its sworn enemy on behalf of Yahweh's
own people. Generation after generation, the
strange turn of the Exodus is reenacted with
new characters, but each time on behalf of
helpless Israel. The narratives do not tell us
all we would like to know about the course
of the battles. But they tell us all Israel needs
to know about Yahweh, which is that Yahweh
is faithful, sovereign, and will not be mocked.
The mode of the power of Yahweh is prophetic speech. The prophets mobilize that power

against the state. The states may have asked cynically, "How may legions does Elisha have?" But against such cynicism toward Yahweh, the narrative answers, "Enough." It is not royal horses and chariots, but the power of Yahweh which ultimately shapes the outcome of the historical process. Clearly we are dealing here with a very different rationality, a rationality which refuses to accommodate royal reason. The narratives have no great attraction to violence, but they also are not embarrassed by what is necessary for survival and well-being.

4. In one other narrative we note the cynicism of the Assyrians who mock Israelite weakness by an offer of two thousand horses if Israel has riders to mount, which obviously Israel does not (II Kings 18:24). The imperial speaker taunts Israel for depending on Egyptian horses and chariots. But the taunt is defeated, for Yahweh takes the challenge and overcomes the Assyrian threat.

In all these liberation narratives, royal monopoly of power is countered. It is countered by the prophetic oracle which discloses unseen and unrecognized horses and chariots (II Kings 6:16-17). It is countered in II Kings 7:6 by the sound of horses and chariots, creat-

ed by Yahweh. It is countered in I Kings 20:28
when Yahweh hands over the Syrians. It is
countered by the powerful angel of Yahweh
(II Kings 19:35). In all these texts, the narrative reveals Yahweh's power which inscrutably and effectively counters hostile, oppressive royal power. The narrative shows Syrian
horses and chariots not to be as powerful as
was assumed. Israel and the Syrians are permitted to see what they had not seen. And for
us, the narrative asserts the reality of Yahweh
in modes for which we are not prepared.

In our consideration of revelation and violence, we have juxtaposed two contrasting
kinds of material. On the one hand, we have
mentioned rather flat, descriptive accounts of
royal power (Ex. 14:9,23, Deut. 20:1, II Sam.
15:1, I Kg. 18:5, 22:4, II Kg. 3:7, 18:23, 23:11).
These texts read like official memos and sound
in their rendering like the cool, detached
reasoning of technique, as perhaps in the
congressional testimony of Caspar Wein-
berger in which everything is obvious, accept-
able, reasonable, taken for granted and not
to be questioned. Such a mode of evidence is
hardly revelatory, for it discloses nothing. It
only states once again the already known.

By contrast the narratives we have considered disclose what was not known. The narrative of I Kings 20:26-30 shows Israel, which seemed to be "like two little flocks of goats," to be powered by Yahweh's response to the mocking, and therefore available for a victory. In II Kings 6:16-17, reality is evoked by a prophetic oracle of "fear not," which ends in an unexpected vision of horses and chariots of Yahweh who seemed to have none. In II Kings 7:16, it is the very sound of horses and chariots that frightened the Syrians. In II Kings 19:35 an angel of Yahweh repels the imperial army. All four stories offer a different mode of presentation, a different epistemology, and a different universe of discourse. This is narrative art which invites to bold, imaginative faith a community that is short on royal technique. But this community is not without its own peculiar rationality which believes that the world is ordered, governed and powered by an authority to which kings do not have access and over which they cannot prevail.

The narratives reveal that faithful imagination is more powerful than dominating technique. The narratives offer a convergence of:

  a) narrative primitivism, which is obligated to explain nothing,
  b) sociological marginality, which cannot rely on human resources,
  c) epistemological naivete, which refuses royal modes of certitude, and
  d) theological amazement, which is innocent and desperate enough to believe, and is not disappointed.

These factors together in the four narratives of I Kings 20:26-30, II Kings 6:16-17, II Kings 7:16, and II Kings 18:19-19:37 are indeed revelatory. They disclose what had not been seen. They make known what had not been known. And when this alternative is known and seen, the sure, managed world of royal technique and certitude is stunningly dismantled. The rulers of this age are marvelously put to flight. Israel's life is rendered in these narratives in an alternative rationality that has power, substance, and reality, all rooted in and derived from this subversive disclosure of Yahweh.

Yahweh's inscrutable competence against royal horses and chariots is echoed in the odd prayer and teaching of Jesus:

> I thank thee, Father, Lord of Heaven and earth, that thou hast hidden these things from the wise and understanding and revealed them to babes; yea, Father, for such was thy gracious will . . .
> Then turning to the disciples he said privately: "Blessed are the eyes which see what you see! For I tell you that many prophets and kings desired to see what you see, and did not see it, and to hear what you hear, and did not hear it" (Luke 10:21-24). [59]

What is hidden from the kings is disclosed to the prophets in Israel. They see and know another kind of power.

We have observed texts that, in a descriptive way, document the inventory of royal chariots. These texts we take either as actual, factual reports, or as polemics against royal power. Secondly, we have observed texts that tell tales of alternative forms of power that triumph over royal instruments of domination. The contrast between the *descriptions of royal domination* and *narratives of alternative forms of power* reflects Israel's alternative reading of the historical process. The mode of expression which contrasts flat description and imaginative narrative corresponds to the modes of power which may be discerned in the historical process. In ancient Israel, the imaginative narrative is characteristically stronger than the descriptive memo. The narrative more nearly articulates the decisive direction of the historical process. That is, the mode of discourse correlates with ways of reality and modes of power. How Israel speaks is related to what Israel trusts in and hopes for. [60]

That contrast between descriptive inventory and imaginative narrative leads to a warning that Israel should not imitate or be seduced by such royal modes of power (cf. Deut. 17:14-20)[61] or royal modes of communication.[62] If Israel imitates the nations or is seduced by their power or their gods, Israel will also become an agent of domination.[63] Israel knows it is not to emulate royal modes of power, knowledge, or language. Israel also knows that alternative modes of power, knowledge, and language are available which permit freedom and justice.

VII

Our study has considered in turn,

a) descriptive inventories of royal domination through horses and chariots,

b) imaginative narratives of alternative power concerning Yahweh's power against horses and chariots,

c) prohibition against imitation and seduction by such horses and chariots.

Israel developed an important and sustained theological tradition which affirmed that the power of Yahweh is stronger than the royal power of horses and chariots. In all parts of the Biblical tradition, it is affirmed that the power of Yahweh will defeat oppressive kings who have horses and chariots. The "power of Yahweh" is not exposited in detail. Obviously the power of Yahweh belongs to a very different, non-royal rationality, but the tradition does not doubt that the power is effective in actual, concrete historical interactions.[64]

The motif of Yahweh's triumph over horses and chariots may be found in three kinds of texts which range over the entire Old Testament literature.

1. Prophetic texts assert the liberating power of God over against royal domination:

    a) I will have pity on the house of Judah, and I will deliver them by the Lord their God; I will not deliver them by bow nor by sword, nor by war, nor by horses, nor by horsemen (Hos. 1:7). [65]

    b) Woe to those who go down to Egypt for help,
       who rely on horses,
       who trust in chariots because they are many
       and in horsemen because they are very strong,
       but do not look to the Holy One of Israel
       or consult the Lord
       (Is. 31:1, cf. v. 3 and 30:15-16). [66]

    c) And in the day, says the Lord,
       I will cut off your horses from among you
       and I will destroy your chariots
       (Micah 5:10). [67]

The text of Micah goes on to speak of destroying cities, sorceries and images,

> And in the anger and wrath will
>   I execute vengeance
> upon the nations that did not obey
> (Micah 5:15).

d) Thus says the Lord
   who makes a way in the sea,
   a path in the mighty waters,
   who brings forth chariot and horse,
   army and warrior,
   they lie down, they cannot rise,
   they are extinguished, quenched
       like a wick (Is. 43:15-17).

This reference alludes to the Exodus and is followed by the remarkable assertion, "Behold, I am doing a new thing," i.e., Yahweh is crushing the horses and chariots of Babylon and so permitting exiled Israel to go home.

e) This is the word of the Lord
       to Zerubbabel:
   not by might, nor by power, but
   by my Spirit, says the Lord of Hosts
   (Zech. 4:6).

To be sure, in this well-known text, horses and chariots are not mentioned, but I consider this statement to be an extension of the same

trajectory. Yahweh's opposition to royal, military power is in this text couched in apocalyptic language. But the claim of Yahweh's governance is the same. Prophetic faith sets the
inscrutable power of Yahweh over against the
pretensions of state power. This paradigmatic
antithesis is acted out already in the Exodus
narrative.[68]

2. In the Psalms, the motif of horses and
chariots is articulated:

a) Some boast of chariots, some
   of horses,
   but we boast in the name of the
   Lord our God (Ps. 20:7).

In this royal Psalm, the contrast between
conventional royal power and the power of
Yahweh is total. The verb "boast" here is a
rendering of *zakar*[69] and so should not be
overinterpreted. But the conventional rendering "boast" suggests a proximity to Jer.
9:22-23 (which in turn is quoted in I Cor.
1:31).[70]

b) A king is not saved by his great army,
   a warrior is not delivered by his
   great strength.

> The war horse is a vain hope
> for victory,
> and by its great strength it
> cannot save (Ps. 33:16-17).
c) At thy rebuke, O God of Jacob,
both rider and horse lay stunned,
But thou, terrible art thou (Ps. 76:6-7).
d) His delight is not in the strength
of the horse
> nor is his pleasure in the legs of a man;
> but the Lord takes pleasure[71] in
> those who fear him
> in those who hope in his steadfast love
> (Ps. 147:10-11).

3. The question of what consitutes power also appears in Proverbs:

> No wisdom, no understanding,
> no counsel
> can avail against the Lord.
> The horse is made ready for the day
> of battle,
> but victory belongs to the Lord
> (Prov. 21:30-31).

von Rad has identified this text along with five others that articulate the hidden, inscru-

table ways of Yahweh's governance which
challenge all human self-security, whether
by way of knowledge, power, planning or
ingenuity.[72]

In all these texts, prophetic assertions
(Hos. 1:7, Is. 31:1, Micah 5:10, Is. 43:15-17,
Zech. 4:6), psalmic doxologies (Ps. 20:7,
33:16-17, 76:6-7, 147:10-11), and sapiential
discernment (Prov. 21:30-31), we have theological statements which are eloquent and not
problematic. In the texts, the difficult issue
of Yahweh's involvement in violence is not
visible. Yet all these texts are rooted in and
derived from the much more primitive statement of Josh. 11:6, "hamstring the horses and
burn the chariots." The other more removed
statements depend on the concreteness of
such a warrant. Yahweh's sovereignty over
horses and chariots is made visible in that concrete action which Yahweh authorizes.

VIII

The theological outcome of Joshua 11 concerns the will and capacity of Yahweh to over-
turn the present historical arrangements of
society which are judged to be inequitable and

against the purposes of Yahweh. Yahweh is here revealed as the true governor of the historical-political process, armed alternatives notwithstanding. At the beginning of the narrative, Israel is assaulted by superior force (v. 1). But by word (v. 6) and by inscrutable, hidden intervention (v. 20), Israel receives its inheritance and rest according to God's promise (v. 23). Yahweh is disclosed as a God who keeps promises within the historical arena. The narrative is a tale of a transformation from domination to inheritance wrought by Yahweh's sovereign will through Israel's bold obedience.

Two texts may be cited that marvelously articulate this strange narrative faith that creates social possibility against a new might. First, at the decisive pause in the land narrative, this encounter takes place. The tribes of Ephraim and Manasseh articulate their weakness in the face of Canaanite chariots:

> The hill country is not enough for us; yet all the Canaanites who dwell in the plain have chariots of iron, both those in Bethshean and its villages and those in the Valley of Jezreel (Josh. 17:16).

Joshua, man of faith, responds with an assurance:

> Then Joshua said to the house of Joseph, to Ephraim and Manasseh, "You are a numerous people, and have great power; you shall not have one lot only, but the hill country shall by yours, for though it is a forest, you shall clear it and possess it to its farthest borders; you shall drive out the Canaanites, though they have chariots of iron, and though they are strong" (vv. 17-18).

It is this summons to faith that makes the difference. The voice of hope is the great equalizer in the historical process.

Second, at the deathbed scene of Elisha (who had considerable experience against horses and chariots), king Joash grieves, because without this prophetic voice of hope he knows he is hopeless and helpless. The king laments:

> My father, my father. The chariots of Israel and its horsemen (II Kings 13:14, cf. 2:12).

The king acknowledges that the prophetic figure of Elisha is Israel's mode of power in the world, the only resource this community has in a world of harsh power.

I conclude with four comments:

1. The fundamental claim of Josh. 11 is that Yahweh is disclosed as a God who will invert the historical process and give land to

the landless. That claim, so far as the tradition is concerned, is beyond dispute. The command against horses and chariots looks back to the defeat of Pharaoh in Ex. 14:6-7, 23 (cf. Ex. 15:1, 21) and Sisera (Jud. 4:3, 7, 13-16)[73] and forward to the defeat of Babylon (Is. 43:16-21), all texts concerning horses and chariots and imperial power. The troublesome part is that Yahweh's transforming governance takes place in such concrete, human ways as hamstringing and burning. Everything hinges on this warrant for action; the faithful act of obedience, so featured in Josh. 11, is response to the permit of Yahweh. In Biblical faith the great gift of deliverance comes in historical concreteness.

2. For the people in the text, we ask, is this really revelation? Does God say such things as in Josh. 11:6? When the permit of Yahweh is embedded in this community of marginality, when revelation is taken as the community's sense of its future with God, this is indeed a disclosure, for it must be so if this community is to have a genuine historical future. None in the community doubted either that God willed such a future, or that the future came at great risk.

3. If revelation is to be always embedded in context, then we must see if this narrative of Joshua is disclosure from God for communities of marginality in our own time which face the great odds of horses and chariots. The affirmation of third world communities of faith is that God's great promise of land and justice is indeed linked to concrete human acts against horses and chariots. As in ancient peasant Israel, none can persuade such communities of faith and hope that the God of justice and freedom withholds such a permit.

4. In our own cultural context, however, we must read the narrative as disclosure "from the other side" within communities of domination. We are more fully embedded in communities of horses and chariots, more fully committed to domination. The narrative, and its trajectory as I have traced it, suggest that such communities of domination have no warrant for arms and control, but that this God in inscrutable ways is aligned against the horses and chariots, working through hardness of heart, until the whole enterprise collapses. The powerful lineage of Pharaoh, Sisera, Nebuchadnezzar never learns in time. But the text persists and is always offered

again. It is a disclosure of hope to those embedded in reliance on horses and chariots, a warning that all such arms cannot secure against God's force for life. This partisan, contextualized disclosure does not regard hamstringing and burning as unacceptable violence. Rather, the disclosure is aimed against domination by the Canaanite. It is maddening that at the crucial places, the text mumbles about how the power of Yahweh could work against such hardware and such technique. But the text, where it mumbles, mumbles because the power of the Spirit cannot be articulated in the rationality of the kings. Indeed, perhaps what is finally disclosed is that the power of God, the rush of the Spirit toward liberation, will never be articulated in the rationality of domination.

From that awareness it is not a very large step to claim that,

> The foolishness of God is wiser than humanity, and the weakness of God is stronger than humanity (I Cor. 1:25).

That insight is already celebrated in Josh. 11, where these land-desperate people watched while the powerful city-kings were

undone by the command, permit, and warrant
of Yahweh. The rhetoric of such a narrative
is not congenial to us in our royal rationality.
It is precisely emancipation from that royal
rationality, however, that lets another mode
of speech render another mode of life,
wrought by a very different kind of power.

NOTES

1. David Tracy, *The Analogical Imagination* (New York: Crossroad, 1981) chapters 3-7, has usefully interpreted this conviction in terms of the Bible as a "classic."

2. See David H. Kelsey, *The Uses of Scripture in Recent Theology* (Philadelphia: Fortress Press, 1975).

3. Jon Sobrino, *The True Church and the Poor* (Maryknoll, NY: Orbis Books, 1984) 10-21, has shown how "the Enlightenment" as a context of interpretation can be handled in two very different ways, depending on whether one organizes the matter around Kant or Marx. Obviously Kant and Marx were interested in very different notions of what may be enlightened and the implications for interpretation lead in very different directions. This difference is illustrative of the interpretive options more generally available.

4. Jürgen Habermas, *Knowledge and Human Interests* (Boston: Beacon Press, 1971) has shown how all knowledge is related to matters of interest, and that any imagined objectivity is likely to be an exercise in self-deception. On such presumed objectivity, see Elisabeth Schüssler Fiorenza, *Bread Not Stone* (Boston: Beacon Press, 1984).

5. See the helpful statement by Donal Dorr, *Spirituality and Justice* (Maryknoll, NY: Orbis Books, 1984) 43-51.

6. On the human person (and derivatively the human community) as a constructor of meanings, see Robert Kegan, *The Evolving Self* (Cambridge: Har-

vard University Press, 1982), and Roy Schafer, *Language and Insight* (New Haven: Yale University Press, 1978).

7. See the summary statement of Robert R. Wilson, *Sociological Approaches to the Old Testament* (Philadelphia: Fortress Press, 1984).

8. A helpful example of how sociological analysis may shape exegetical interpretation is offered in *God of the Lowly,* ed. by Willy Schottroff and Wolfgang Stegemann (Maryknoll, NY: Orbis Books, 1984).

9. Norman K. Gottwald, *The Tribes of Yahweh* (Maryknoll NY: Orbis Books, 1979).

10. Robert R. Wilson, *Prophecy and Society in Ancient Israel* (Philadelphia: Fortress Press, 1979).

11. Paul D. Hanson, *The Dawn of Apocalyptic* (Philadelphia: Fortress Press, 1975).

12. See Kuno Füssel, "The Materialist Reading of the Bible," *The Bible and Liberation,* ed. by Norman K. Gottwald (Maryknoll, NY: Orbis Books, 1983), 134-46, and more generally, Michel Clevenot, *Materialist Approaches to the Bible* (Maryknoll, NY: Orbis Books, 1985).

13. Leonard Boff, *Church: Charisma and Power* (New York: Crossroad, 1985) 110-115, has applied these categories to the sacramental life of the church, even as Füssel has applied them to the character of the text.

14. For a critical assessment of this interpretive view as it pertains to Biblical interpretation, see John Barton, *Reading the Old Testament: Method in Biblical Study* (Philadelphia: Westminister Press, 1984).

15. Ricoeur's work is scattered in many places, but see especially *Interpretation Theory* (Fort Worth: Texas Christian University Press, 1976); *The Conflict of Interpretations* (Evanston: Northwestern University Press, 1974); *The Philosophy of Paul Ricoeur,* ed. by Charles E. Reagan and David Steward (Boston: Beacon Press, 1978), and *Semeia* 4 (1975).

16. For a most helpful introduction to Wilder's view of literature as world-making, see Wilder, "Story and Story-World," *Interpretation* 37 (1983) 353-64.

17. David M. Gunn, *The Fate of King Saul* (JSOT Supp. 14: Sheffield: University of Sheffield, 1980), and *The Story of King David* (JSOT Supp. 6: Sheffield: University of Sheffield, 1978).

18. See especially David J.A. Clines, *I, He, We & They* (JSOT Supp. 1: Sheffield: University of Sheffield, 1978).

19. Phyllis Trible, *God and the Rhetoric of Sexuality* (Philadelphia: Fortress Press, 1978) and *Texts of Terror* (Philadelphia: Fortress Press, 1984).

20. Milton L. Myers, *The Soul of a Modern Economic Man* (Chicago: University of Chicago Press, 1983), has shown how the work of Hobbes is "the text" for Adam Smith, which in turn has become the text for the capitalist world, even if unacknowledged.

21. On the active power of "sense-making" as the production of sense, see David Jobling, *The Sense of Biblical Narrative* (JSOT Supp. 7: Sheffield: University of Sheffield, 1978), especially 1-3; and Walter Brueggemann, "As the Text 'Makes Sense'," *The Christian Ministry* 14 (Nov., 1983) 7-10.

22. See my attempt at such a methodological interface in *David's Truth* (Philadelphia: Fortress Press, 1985).

23. On the general question, see Patrick D. Miller, Jr.,
     "God the Warrior," *Interpretation* 19 (1965) 39-46;
     Paul D. Hanson, "War and Peace in the Hebrew
     Bible, *Interpretation* 38 (1984) 341-62; Diane Ber-
     gant, "Peace in a Universe of Order," *Biblical and
     Theological Reflections on "The Challenge of Peace,"*
     ed. by John T. Pawlikowski and Donald Senior
     (Wilmington, DE: Michael Glazier, Inc., 1984) 17-30;
     H. Eberhard von Waldow, "The Concept of War in
     the Old Testament," *Horizons in Biblical Theology*
     6 (1984) 27-48. The journals in which the Hanson and
     von Waldow articles appear have entire issues
     devoted to the subject of war and peace in the Bible.
     Most recently see Robert M. Good, "The Just War
     in Ancient Israel," *JBL* 104 (1985) 385-400.

24. For a summary of the critical discussion, see
     Brevard H. Childs, *Introduction to the Old Testa-
     ment as Scripture* (Philadelphia: Fortress Press,
     1979) 241-44.

25. Cf. Albrecht Alt, "Josua," *Werden und Wesen des
     Alten Testaments,* ed. by F. Stummer and J. Hempel
     (BZAW 66; Berlin: A Töpelmann, 1936, reprinted
     in *Kleine Schriften zur Geschichte des Volkes Israel
     I* (Munich: C.H. Beck, 1953) 176-92.

26. We will consider both parts of the chapter in order
     to attend to the dynamics of the text. In critical
     analysis, the first part of the chapter is a specific
     narrative, whereas the latter part is a general theo-
     logical summary. Literarily the two parts serve very
     different functions.

27. See Robert G. Boling and G. Ernest Wright, *Joshua*
     (AB 6: Garden City, NY: Doubleday and Co., Inc., 1982)
     303-314, for the notion of a two-stage presentation of
     the conquest. See the general discussion of Martin
     Noth, *The Deuteronomistic History* (JSOT Supp. 15:
     Sheffield: University of Sheffield, 1981) 36-41.

28. See Boling and Wright, *op. cit.*, 303.

29. Norman K. Gottwald, *The Tribes of Yahweh* (Maryknoll, NY: Orbis Books, 1979) 389-419. See also George E. Mendenhall, "The Hebrew Conquest of Palestine," BAR 3 (1970) 100-120.

30. See Gottwald, *The Tribes of Yahweh* 542-43. Boling and Wright, *op. cit.*, 307, suggest only that chariots are "new-fangled" and therefore Israel did not have them. I suggest that such a chronological explanation misses the point of the theological and sociological practice to which Israel is committed.

31. Boling and Wright, *op. cit.*, 316, consider this as belonging to Dtr.; Noth, *op. cit.*, 38, refers to a "compiler" and assigns 20b to Dtr. For our purposes, such a refinement of literary analysis is neither necessary nor useful.

32. Robert Polzin, *Moses and the Deuteronomist* (New York: Seabury Books) 123-26.

33. Norman K. Gottwald, "Social History of the United Monarchy," (paper read to the SBL Seminar on Sociology of the "monarchy," December 20, 1983).

34. Boling, *op. cit.*, 310, comes close to such a conclusion when he speaks of "the royal families and ruling aristocracies," and then of the "peasants." He has not, in my judgment, pursued far enough the implications of such a social analysis.

35. Edgar W. Conrad, "The 'Fear Not' Oracles in Second Isaiah," VT 34 (1984) 129-152, has greatly contributed to our understanding of this genre of speech. See more extensively Edgar W. Conrad, *Fear Not Warrior* (Brown Judaic Studies 75; Chico, Calif.: Scholars Press, 1985). Conrad has shown how the formula may yield either an assurance or a command. In our text, it yields both. Cf. pp. 8-10.

36.   On the function and power of the particle *kî,* see
      James Muilenburg, "The Linguistic and Rhetorical
      Usages of the Particle *kî* in the Old Testament,"
      Hearing and Speaking the Word, ed. by Thomas F.
      Best (Chico, CA: Scholars Press, 1984) 208-33.

37.   On the psychology of granting and receiving per-
      mission, see Eric Berne, *What Do You Say After
      You Say Hello?* (New York: Bantam Books, 1972)
      123-25; and *Beyond Games and Scripts* (New York:
      Ballantine Books, 1976) 399, for a definition of the
      term in the context of one theory of therapy. "The
      Granting of Permission" can be done by one in
      authority to authorize another to act in freedom and
      courage against old patterns of coercion and repres-
      sion. My colleague, John Quigley, has helped find
      these references and has also helped me see the
      dangerous distortion of the notion in popular usage
      with reference to ideological autonomy, which gives
      "permission" to do what one wants. But free of this
      distortion, I suggest the notion illuminates our pas-
      sage and the revelatory speech of Yahweh. The
      Israelites, on any sociological analysis, were disad-
      vantaged and oppressed. The "permit of Yahweh"
      authorized this community to act by "hamstringing
      and burning" for the sake of their own social destiny.
      Without such "permission," they would have con-
      tinued in their oppressed, marginalized condition.
      Such revelatory permission is a counterpart to the
      "revolutionary impetus" of these narratives.

38.   On the monopoly of interpretation, the power and the
      problems it yields, see Frank Kermode, *The Art of
      Telling* (Cambridge: Harvard University Press, 1983).

39.   On the doing of theology that is embedded in local
      community experience, see Robert S. Schreiter,
      Constructing Local Theologies (Maryknoll, NY: Orbis
      Books, 1985).

40. There is of course a methodological problem with making old memory a part of revelation, because it leaves open the charge of infinite regress. When one finally reaches the event behind which there is no old memory, that event is no doubt a theophany. On the reality of older memory in the faith of Israel, see the proposal of Gottwald, *op. cit.*, 483-97 and *passim*.

41. Methodologically it is the peasant yearning which is the new and decisive ingredient in our understanding. It is this yearning publicly expressed which evokes the old memory in its powerful authority and mobilizes the present leadership also accepted as authoritative.

42. H. Richard Niebuhr, *The Meaning of Revelation* (New York: The Macmillan Company, 1962).

43. John L. McKenzie, "The Social Character of Inspiration," CBQ 24 (1962) 115-24.

44. The general notion of Niebuhr and McKenzie is inadequate because they did not reckon with the particularity of the community and therefore the particularity of its revelation. Each community operates through a particular rationality. By ignoring the socio-economic particularity of a community, communities of marginality are likely to be thought of as irrational, so that their claim to have revelation is discredited. This dismissal of marginality as a habitat for revelation operates both sociologically and psychologically. On the latter, see Brian W. Grant, *Schizophrenia: A Source of Social Insight* (Philadelphia: Westminster Press, 1975), who considers that the insights of schizophrenics may be revelational, even if an odd rationality which people with "horses and chariots" are likely to misunderstand and dismiss.

45.   On the problematic of "act of God," see Gordon D. Kaufman, "On the Meaning of 'Act of God'," HTR 61 (1968) 175-201.

46.   See my chapter, "Blessed are the History-Makers," in *Hope Within History,* forthcoming, John Knox Press. I have argued that "history-making" depends on vulnerability. Those who move from coercive strength are characteristically "history-stoppers" because they want to stop the ongoing conversation about power.

47.   It is interesting that in the stylized catalogues of blessings bestowed by God, horses are never listed in such a recital (cf. Job 42:12-16, Deut. 11:15, 28:4, Josh. 1:14, II Kings 3:17). Whereas cattle belong in such a list, horses regularly are treated as an imposition upon a community by an occupying force, but not as a gift to be treasured in the community. Horses are characteristically threats, not prizes or treasures.

48.   Polzin, *op. cit.,* 113-24.

49.   On the criticism of this text, see Alexander Rofé, "The Laws of Warfare in the Book of Deuteronomy," JSOT 32 (1985) 28-39.

50.   On the sociology and power of rage in situations of oppression, see Frank A. Spina, *The Concept of Social Rage in the Old Testament and the Ancient Near East* (unpublished dissertation, University of Michigan, 1977).

51.   Gottwald, *op. cit.,* 490-96, identifies the Levites as the revolutionary cadre who carry this news of the liberation of Yahweh. Mendenhall, in more "realistic" fashion, urged that the news of Exodus was carried specifically by Joshua and Caleb.

52. On the problematic of this theological theme, von Rad, *Old Testament Theology II* (New York: Harper and Row, 1965) 151-55, and Brevard S. Childs, *The Book of Exodus* (Philadelphia: Westminster Press, 1974) 170-75.

53. Boling and Wright, *op. cit.*, 307, conclude, "Such military efficiency reflects a feudal system in which the charioteers, or *maryanu*, belong to a class enjoying special privileges and performing special services for the king." Gottwald, *op. cit.*, 543, writes, "Hamstringing horses and burning chariots were defensive measures against the hated and feared superior weaponry of the enemy."

54. Clearly Solomon's monarchy embodies much that repelled the Israel of Moses and Joshua. See Mendenhall, "The Monarchy," *Interpretation* 29 (1975) 155-170.

55. The different sociology of these texts needs to be correlated with the different mode of literary expression in which it is reported. Thus the positive assertion of royal power is characteristically reported in lists, inventories, and memos. By contrast, the alternative power of Yahweh does not come articulated in such controlled modes of expression, but in narratives of a playful kind which allow for surprise and inscrutability. The modes of power are matched to ways of speech and to the different epistemologies and rationalities practiced by the speech forms.

56. The formula "I will give" is characteristically the way of victory, as we have seen it also in Josh. 11:6. On the formula, see the comment of von Rad, *Der Heilige Krieg im alten Israel* (Göttingen: Vandenhoeck und Ruprecht, 1958) 7. The phrase promises everything but tells nothing.

57. The formula is the same as in Josh. 11:6.

58.   The seizure of spoil from the strong ones now
       defeated by Yahweh is parallel to Josh. 11.

59.   On the peculiar character of this saying, see M. Jack
       Suggs, *Wisdom, Christology and Law in St. Mat-
       thew's Gospel* (Cambridge: Harvard University
       Press, 1970).

60.   Gail O'Day, *Irony and the Johannine Theology of
       Revelation* (unpublished dissertation, Emory Uni-
       versity, 1983) has shown that the *Wie* of presenta-
       tion is as important as *Dass* and *Was* for under-
       standing this literature as revelatory.

61.   The basis of *ḥerem* is not that Israel should not
       possess, but that Israel should not be seduced. I am
       not sure if Polzin has recognized this difference.

62.   On the seduction of royal modes of communication,
       the substantive issue is the loss of narrative, em-
       barrassment over storytelling and the recasting of
       reality into technical modes of communication. On
       this general seduction and its social outcome, see
       Hans Frei, *The Eclipse of Biblical Narrative* (New
       Haven: Yale University Press, 1974).

63.   The seductive economics of Solomon goes along with
       the changed modes of communication. In contrast
       to David, it is telling that we have no narratives of
       Solomon in the sense that we have them about
       David. One may say that Solomon got horses and
       chariots and lost narrative. I suggest we will not
       understand what is at issue in our present society
       of militarism until we see the connection between
       modes of power and modes of speech.

64.   On the power of Yahweh articulated as "the hand
       of Yahweh," see P.D. Miller, Jr. and J.J.M. Roberts,
       The Hand of the Lord (Baltimore: Johns Hopkins
       University Press, 1977).

64. On the power of Yahweh articulated as "the hand of Yahweh," se P.D. Miller, Jr. and J.J.M. Roberts, *The Hand of the Lord* (Baltimore: Johns Hopkins University Press, 1977).

65. On this verse, see H.W. Wolff, *Hosea* (Hermeneia: Philadelphia: Fortress Press, 1974) 20-21.

66. On the issue of faith in Isaiah, see von Rad, *Old Testament Theology II,* 158-69. An investigation of the term *baṭaḥ* in the tradition of Isaiah would be worth pursuing.

67. One can understand the polemic of the Micah tradition if one accepts the sociological analysis of Wolff that Micah is the voice of the small rural landowner always resistant to imperial impingement. Cf. Hans Walter Wolff, "Micah the Moreshite – The Prophet and his Background," *Israelite Wisdom,* ed. by John G. Gammie, (Missoula, MT: Scholars Press, 1978) 77-84. Delbert Hillers, *Micah* (Hermeneia: Philadelphia: Fortress Press, 1984) 72-74, interprets Micah's oracle as a renunciation of all that destroys Israel's true identity.

68. The contrast between the power of Yahweh and the pretensions of state power is nicely drawn in I Sam. 17:45 and the encompassing narrative. See my discussion in *David's Truth,* in which I have drawn attention to the epistemology of the tribe which is articulated to claim a zone of freedom against a hostile state.

69. The use of the term *zakar* here is peculiar. Its conventional rendering of "boast" is surely correct, but perhaps it also linked the present doxology to concrete memories of the triumphs of Yahweh in the past, which were won against great odds. It is the memory that permits the doxology.

70. The verb in Jer. 9:22-23 is *halal.* On the text from
     Jeremiah, see Brueggemann, "The Epistemological
     Crisis of Israel's Two Histories (Jer. 9:22-23),"
     Israelite Wisdom, 85-105.

71. The verb *ḥapaṣ* used here is the same as in Jer. 9:23.

72. von Rad, *Old Testament Theology I* (New York:
     Harper and Row, 1962) 438-41; *Wisdom in Israel*
     (Nashville: Abingdon Press, 1972) 97-110.

73. Gottwald has established a model of interpretation
     which takes Moses and Joshua together. He has
     treated as continuous the Egyptian empire and the
     Canaanite city-state as metaphors of oppression. In
     Josh. 4:23, it is evident that the cultic tradition
     labored to establish the same equation.

The Pere Marquette Theology Lectures

1969: "The Authority for Authority,"
by Quentin Quesnell
Professor of Theology
Marquette University

1970: "Mystery and Truth,"
by John Macquarrie
Professor of Theology
Union Theological Seminary, New York

1971: "Doctrinal Pluralism,"
by Bernard Lonergan, S.J.
Professor of Theology
Regis College, Ontario

1972: "Infallibility,"
by George A. Lindbeck
Professor of Theology
Yale University

1973: "Ambiguity in Moral Choice,"
by Richard A. McCormick, S.J.
Professor of Moral Theology
Bellarmine School of Theology

1974: "Church Membership as a Catholic
and Ecumenical Problem,"
by Avery Dulles, S.J.
Professor of Theology
Woodstock College

1975: "The Contributions of Theology to
Medical Ethics,"
by James Gustafson
University Professor of Theological Ethics
University of Chicago

1976: "Religious Values in an Age of Violence,"
by Rabbi Marc Tanenbaum
Director of National Interreligious Affairs
American Jewish Committee, New York City

1977: "Truth Beyond Relativism: Karl Mannheim's Sociology of Knowledge,"
by Gregory Baum
Professor of Theology and Religious Studies
St. Michael's College

1978: "A Theology of 'Uncreated Energies'"
by George A. Maloney, S.J.
Professor of Theology
John XXIII Center For Eastern Christian Studies
Fordham University

1980: "Method in Theology: An Organon For Our Time,"
by Frederick E. Crowe, S.J.
Research Professor in Theology
Regis College, Toronto

1981: "Catholics in the Promised Land of the Saints,"
by James Hennesey, S.J.
Professor of the History of Christianity
Boston College

1982: "Whose Experience Counts in Theological Reflection?"
by Monika Hellwig
Professor of Theology
Georgetown University

1983: "The Theology and Setting of Discipleship in the Gospel of Mark,"
by John R. Donahue, S.J.
Professor of Theology
Jesuit School of Theology, Berkeley

1984: "Should War be Eliminated? Philosophical and Theological Investigations,"
by Stanley Hauerwas
Professor of Theology
Notre Dame University

1985   "From Vision to Legislation:
        From the Council to a Code of Laws,"
        by Ladislas M. Orsy, S.J.
        Professor of Canon Law
        Catholic University of America
        Washington, D.C.

1986   "Revelation and Violence:
        A Study in Contextualization,"
        by Walter Brueggemann
        Professor of Old Testament
        Eden Theological Seminary
        St. Louis, Missouri

Uniform format, cover and binding.

Copies of this Lecture and the others in the series are obtainable from:

Marquette University Press
Marquette University
Milwaukee, Wisconsin 53233, U.S.A.